Greenmarket Tote

Easy

MEASUREMENTS
Circumference Approx 35"/89cm
Height (excluding strap) Approx 15½"/39.5cm

MATERIALS
Yarn
LION BRAND® 24/7 Cotton®, 3½oz/100g balls, each approx
186yd/170m (mercerized cotton) (4)
• 3 balls of #172 Grass

Hook
• One size G-6 (4.25mm) crochet hook, *or size to obtain gauges*

Notions
• Stitch markers
• Tapestry needle

GAUGES
• 16 sc + 16 rnds = approx 4"/10cm using size G-6 (4.25mm)
crochet hook.
• 6 (sc, ch 3) reps = approx 4"/10cm in Rnds 1–31 of body using
size G-6 (4.25mm) crochet hook.
BE SURE TO CHECK YOUR GAUGES.

STITCH GLOSSARY
sc2tog (sc 2 sts together) [Insert hook in next st and draw up a
loop] twice, yarn over and draw through all 3 loops on hook—1 st
decreased.

NOTES
1) Tote is worked in one piece.
2) Base is worked first in continuous rnds (spiral) of sc. Body is worked
in joined rnds of (sc, ch 3) and (sc, ch 5) mesh. One end of strap is
worked directly onto top edge of the Tote; other end of strap is sewn
to the Tote.

TOTE
Base
Wrap yarn around index finger. Insert hook into ring on finger, yarn
over and draw up a loop. Carefully slip ring from finger and work the
sts of Rnd 1 into the ring. When Rnd 1 is complete, gently but firmly,
pull tail to tighten center of ring.

Rnd 1 (RS) Ch 1, 6 sc in ring; work in continuous rnds (spiral), do *not*
join last st to first st.
Place a marker in the last sc made to indicate end of rnd. Move
marker up as each rnd is completed.
Rnd 2 Work 2 sc in each sc around—you will have 12 sc in this rnd.
Rnd 3 *Sc in next st, 2 sc in next st; rep from * around—18 sc.
Rnd 4 *Sc in next 2 sts, 2 sc in next st; rep from * around—24 sc.
Rnd 5 *Sc in next 3 sts, 2 sc in next st; rep from * around—30 sc.
Rnd 6 *Sc in next 4 sts, 2 sc in next st; rep from * around—36 sc.
Rnd 7 *Sc in next 5 sts, 2 sc in next st; rep from * around—42 sc.
Rnd 8 *Sc in next 6 sts, 2 sc in next st; rep from * around—48 sc.
Rnd 9 *Sc in next 7 sts, 2 sc in next st; rep from * around—54 sc.
Rnd 10 *Sc in next 8 sts, 2 sc in next st; rep from * around—60 sc.
Rnd 11 *Sc in next 9 sts, 2 sc in next st; rep from * around—66 sc.
Rnd 12 *Sc in next 10 sts, 2 sc in next st; rep from * around—72 sc.
Rnd 13 *Sc in next 11 sts, 2 sc in next st; rep from * around—78 sc.
Rnd 14 *Sc in next 12 sts, 2 sc in next st; rep from * around—84 sc.

Rnd 15 *Sc in next 13 sts, 2 sc in next st; rep from * around—90 sc.

Rnd 16 *Sc in next 14 sts, 2 sc in next st; rep from * around—96 sc.

Rnd 17 *Sc in next 15 sts, 2 sc in next st; rep from * around—102 sc.

Rnd 18 *Sc in next 16 sts, 2 sc in next st; rep from * around—108 sc.

Rnd 19 Sc in each st around.

Body

Mesh Rnd 1 (RS) *Sc in next sc, ch 3, sk next sc; rep from * around; join with sl st in first sc—54 sc and 54 ch-3 sps. Remove end of rnd marker.

Rnds 2–30 Sl st in first ch-3 sp, ch 1, sc in same ch-3 sp, *ch 3, sk next sc, sc in next ch-3 sp; rep from * to last sc, ch 3, sk last sc; join with sl st in first sc—54 sc and 54 ch-3 sps.

Rnd 31 Sl st in first ch-3 sp, ch 1, sc in same ch-3 sp, *ch 5, sk next ch-3 sp, sc in next ch-3 sp; rep from * to last ch-3 sp, ch 5, sk last ch-3 sp; join with sl st in first sc—27 sc and 27 ch-5 sps.

Rnds 32–34 Sl st in first ch-5 sp, ch 1, sc in same ch-5 sp, *ch 5, sk next sc, sc in next ch-5 sp; rep from * to last sc, ch 5, sk last sc; join with sl st in first sc—27 sc and 27 ch-5 sps.

Rnd 35 Ch 1, 4 sc in each ch-5 sp around; join with sl st in first sc—108 sc.

Rnd 36 Ch 1, sc in each st around; join with sl st in first sc.

Strap

Row 1 (RS) Ch 1, sc in first 17 sts.

Decrease Row 2 (WS) Ch 1, turn, sc in first st, sc2tog, sc in each st to last 3 sts, sc2tog, sc in last st—15 sc.

Row 3 Ch 1, turn, sc in each st across.

Row 4 Rep Row 2—13 sc.

Rows 5–8 Rep Rows 3 and 4 twice—9 sc in Row 8.

Row 9 Ch 1, turn, sc in each st across.

Rep Row 9 until strap measures about 24"/61cm from beg, end with a RS row as the last row you work.

Increase Row (WS) Ch 1, turn, sc in first st, 2 sc in next st, sc in each st to last 2 sts, 2 sc in next st, sc in last st—11 sc.

Next Row Ch 1, turn, sc in each st across.

Rep last 2 rows 3 more times—17 sc.

Fasten off.

FINISHING

Sew end of strap to top edge of Tote, on side opposite the beginning of the strap.

Weave in ends.•

Siesta Key Bag

Easy

MEASUREMENTS
Circumference Approx 34"/86.5cm
Height (including straps) Approx 19"/48.5cm

MATERIALS
Yarn
LION BRAND® Rewind, 3½oz/100g balls, each approx 219yd/200m (polyester/viscose) **(5)**
• 1 ball each in #138 Current Situation (A) and #174 Olive You (B)

Hook
• One size K-10½ (6.5mm) crochet hook, *or size to obtain gauge*

Notions
• Tapestry needle

GAUGE
13 sc = approx 4"/10cm using size K-10½ (6.5mm) crochet hook.
BE SURE TO CHECK YOUR GAUGE.

STITCH GLOSSARY
beg-Cl (beginning cluster) Ch 3, yarn over, insert hook in indicated st and draw up a loop, yarn over and draw through 2 loops on hook (2 loops rem on hook); yarn over, insert hook in same st and draw up a loop, yarn over and draw through 2 loops on hook, yarn over and draw through all 3 loops on hook.
Cl (cluster) Yarn over, insert hook in indicated st, yarn over and draw up a loop, yarn over and draw through 2 loops on hook (2 loops rem on hook), [yarn over, insert hook in same st, yarn over and draw up a loop, yarn over and draw through 2 loops on hook] twice; yarn over and draw through all 4 loops on hook.

NOTES
1) Bag is worked in one piece in 3 sections: Base, body, and straps.
2) All sections are worked in joined rnds with the right side always facing.
3) To change yarn color and join at end of a rnd, insert hook in top of beg ch or first st, yarn over with new color and draw through all loops on hook to complete joining sl st. Proceed with new color.

BAG
Base
With A, ch 4; join with sl st in first ch to form a ring.

Rnd 1 Ch 1, make 6 sc in ring; sl st in first sc to join.
Rnd 2 Ch 1, work 2 sc in each of the 6 sc around; join with sl st in first sc—you will have 12 sc in this rnd.
Note Always work the first st of each rnd in the same st as the join.
Rnd 3 Ch 1, *sc in next st, 2 sc in next st, rep from * around, join with sl st in first sc—18 sc.
Rnd 4 Ch 1, *sc in next 2 sts, 2 sc in next st; rep from * around; join with sl st in first sc—24 sc.
Rnd 5 Ch 1, *sc in next 3 sts, 2 sc in next st; rep from * around; join with sl st in first sc—30 sc.
Rnd 6 Ch 1, *sc in next 4 sts, 2 sc in next st; rep from * around; join with sl st in first sc—36 sc.

Rnd 7 Ch 1, *sc in next 5 sts, 2 sc in next st; rep from * around; join with sl st in first sc—42 sc.

Rnd 8 Ch 1, *sc in next 6 sts, 2 sc in next st; rep from * around; join with sl st in first sc—48 sc.

Rnd 9 Ch 1, *sc in next 7 sts, 2 sc in next st; rep from * around; join with sl st in first sc—54 sc.

Rnd 10 Ch 1, *sc in next 8 sts, 2 sc in next st; rep from * around; join with sl st in first sc—60 sc.

Rnd 11 Ch 1, *sc in next 9 sts, 2 sc in next st; rep from * around; join with sl st in first sc—66 sc.

Rnd 12 Ch 1, *sc in next 10 sts, 2 sc in next st; rep from * around; join with sl st in first sc—72 sc.

Rnd 13 Ch 1, *sc in next 11 sts, 2 sc in next st; rep from * around; join with sl st in first sc—78 sc.

Rnd 14 Ch 1, *sc in next 12 sts, 2 sc in next st; rep from * around; join with sl st in first sc—84 sc.

Rnd 15 Ch 1, *sc in next 13 sts, 2 sc in next st; rep from * around; join with sl st in first sc—90 sc.

Rnd 16 Ch 1, *sc in next 14 sts, 2 sc in next st; rep from * around; join with sl st in first sc—96 sc.

Rnd 17 Ch 1, *sc in next 15 sts, 2 sc in next st; rep from * around; join with sl st in first sc—102 sc.

Rnd 18 Ch 1, *sc in next 16 sts, 2 sc in next st; rep from * around; join with sl st in first sc—108 sc.

Body

Rnd 1 With A, beg-Cl in same st as join, *ch 1, sk next st, Cl in next st; rep from * to last st, ch 1, sk last st; join with sl st in top of beg ch-3 and change to B—54 clusters and 54 ch-1 sps. Cut A.

Rnd 2 With B, ch 1, 2 sc in each ch-1 sp around; join with sl st in first sc—108 sc.

Rnd 3–8 With B, ch 1, sc in each st around; join with sl st in first sc.

Change to A at end of Rnd 8. Carry B on wrong side of work until next needed.

Rep Rnds 1–8 for 3 more times. Fasten off B.

Straps

Set-Up Rnd With A, ch 1, sc in next 13 sts, ch 30, sk next 28 sts for first strap, sc in next 26 sts, ch 30, sk next 28 sts for second strap, sc in last 13 sts; join with sl st in first sc—52 sc and 2 ch-30 sps.

Next Rnd Ch 1, sc in each sc and ch around; join with sl st in first sc—112 sc.

Rnds 3–5 Ch 1, sc in each st around; join with sl st in first sc.

Fasten off.

FINISHING

Weave in ends. •

Bushwick Market Bag

●●●
Intermediate

MEASUREMENTS
Circumference Approx 26"/66cm
Height Approx 12½"/32cm

MATERIALS
Yarn
LION BRAND® 24/7 Cotton®, 3½oz/100g balls, each approx
186yd/170m (mercerized cotton)
• 2 balls in #122 Taupe

Hook
• One size G-6 (4.25mm) crochet hook, *or size to obtain gauges*

Notions
• Stitch markers
• Tapestry needle

GAUGES
• 16 sc + 16 rnds = approx 4"/10cm using size G-6 (4.25mm)
crochet hook.
• 4 (sc, ch 3) reps = approx 2½"/6.5cm in Rnds 1–31 of body using
size G-6 (4.25mm) crochet hook.
BE SURE TO CHECK YOUR GAUGES.

NOTES
1) Bag is worked in one piece.
2) Base is worked first in continuous rnds (spiral) of sc. Body is worked
in joined rnds of (sc, ch 3) mesh. Straps are worked last in continuous
rnds (spiral).

BAG
Base
Wrap yarn around index finger. Insert hook into ring on finger, yarn
over and draw up a loop. Carefully slip ring from finger and work the
sts of Rnd 1 into the ring. When Rnd 1 is complete, gently but firmly,
pull tail to tighten center of ring.
Rnd 1 (RS) Ch 1, 6 sc in ring; work in continuous rnds (spiral), do not
join last st to first st.
Place a marker in the last sc made to indicate end of rnd. Move
marker up as each rnd is completed.
Rnd 2 Work 2 sc in each sc around—12 sc.
Rnd 3 *Sc in next st, 2 sc in next st; rep from * around—18 sc.

Rnd 4 *Sc in next 2 sts, 2 sc in next st; rep from * around—24 sc.
Rnd 5 *Sc in next 3 sts, 2 sc in next st; rep from * around—30 sc.
Rnd 6 *Sc in next 4 sts, 2 sc in next st; rep from * around—36 sc.
Rnd 7 *Sc in next 5 sts, 2 sc in next st; rep from * around—42 sc.
Rnd 8 *Sc in next 6 sts, 2 sc in next st; rep from * around—48 sc.
Rnd 9 *Sc in next 7 sts, 2 sc in next st; rep from * around—54 sc.
Rnd 10 *Sc in next 8 sts, 2 sc in next st; rep from * around—60 sc.
Rnd 11 *Sc in next 9 sts, 2 sc in next st; rep from * around—66 sc.
Rnd 12 *Sc in next 10 sts, 2 sc in next st; rep from * around—72 sc.
Rnd 13 *Sc in next 11 sts, 2 sc in next st; rep from * around—78 sc.
Rnd 14 *Sc in next 12 sts, 2 sc in next st; rep from * around—84 sc.
Rnd 15 Sc in each st around.

Body
Rnd 1 (Mesh—RS) *Sc in next sc, ch 3, sk next sc; rep from *
around; join with sl st in first sc—42 sc and 42 ch-3 sps. Remove end
of rnd marker.
Rnds 2–31 Sl st in first ch-3 sp, ch 1, sc in same ch-3 sp, *ch 3,
sk next sc, sc in next ch-3 sp; rep from * to last sc, ch 3, sk last sc;
join with sl st in first sc—42 sc and 42 ch-3 sps.
Rnd 32 Ch 1, 2 sc in each ch-3 sp around; join with sl st in
first sc—84 sc.
Rnd 33 Ch 1, sc in each st around; join with sl st in first sc.

Shape Straps
Rnd 1 (RS) Sc in first st, ch 80 for strap, sk next 18 sts, sc in next 24
sts, ch 80 for strap, sk next 18 sts, sc in each of next 23 sts—48 sc
and 2 ch-80 sps (two 24-sc groups separated by ch-80 sps).
Place a marker in the last sc made to indicate end of rnd. Move
marker up as each rnd is completed.
Rnd 2 Sc in each st and ch around—208 sc.
Rnds 3 and 4 Sc in each st around.
Rnd 5 (WS) Ch 1, turn, sl st in each next st around.
Fasten off.

FINISHING
Edging
From WS, join yarn with sl st in any ch at inside corner of one strap.
Work sl st evenly spaced along edge of strap and top edge of Bag.
Fasten off.
Rep edging on opposite side of Bag.

Weave in ends.•

Encantada Crochet Bag

Easy

MEASUREMENTS
Circumference Approx 27"/68.5cm
Height Approx 14½"/37cm

MATERIALS
Yarn
LION BRAND® 24/7 Cotton®, 3½oz/100g balls, each approx
186yd/170m (mercerized cotton) (4)
• 2 balls each in #178 Jade (A) and #156 Mint (B)

Hook
• One size F-5 (3.75mm) crochet hook, *or size to obtain gauge*

Notions
• Stitch markers
• Tapestry needle

GAUGE
21 sc + 17 rnds = approx 4"/10cm using size F-5 (3.75mm)
crochet hook.
BE SURE TO CHECK YOUR GAUGE.

NOTES
1) Bag is worked in one piece in continuous rnds (spiral).
2) Base of Bag is worked with A only. Body of Bag is worked with
A and B, changing color following Color Chart.
3) To change yarn color, work last st of old color to last yarn over.
Yarn over with new color and draw through all loops on hook to
complete st. Proceed with new color. Do *not* fasten off old color.
Carry color not in use under sts of current color.
4) The drawstring is worked separately, then threaded through
ch-3 eyelets and sewn to last rnd of Bag Base to make shoulder
straps. A diagram is provided to help with the sewing!

BAG
Base
Wrap A around index finger. Insert hook into ring on finger, yarn over
and draw up a loop. Carefully slip ring from finger and work the sts
of Rnd 1 into the ring. When Rnd 1 is complete, gently but firmly,
pull tail to tighten center of ring.
Rnd 1 (RS) Ch 1, 6 sc in ring; work in continuous rnds (spiral), do not
join last st to first st.

Place a marker in the last sc made to indicate end of rnd. Move
marker up as each rnd is completed.
Rnd 2 Work 2 sc in each sc around—you will have 12 sc in this rnd.
Rnd 3 *Sc in next st, 2 sc in next st; rep from * around—18 sc.
Rnd 4 *Sc in next 2 sts, 2 sc in next st; rep from * around—24 sc.
Rnd 5 *Sc in next 3 sts, 2 sc in next st; rep from * around—30 sc.
Rnd 6 *Sc in next 4 sts, 2 sc in next st; rep from * around—36 sc.
Rnd 7 *Sc in next 5 sts, 2 sc in next st; rep from * around—42 sc.
Rnd 8 *Sc in next 6 sts, 2 sc in next st; rep from * around—48 sc.
Rnd 9 *Sc in next 7 sts, 2 sc in next st; rep from * around—54 sc.
Rnd 10 *Sc in next 8 sts, 2 sc in next st; rep from * around—60 sc.
Rnd 11 *Sc in next 9 sts, 2 sc in next st; rep from * around—66 sc.
Rnd 12 *Sc in next 10 sts, 2 sc in next st; rep from * around—72 sc.
Rnd 13 *Sc in next 11 sts, 2 sc in next st; rep from * around—78 sc.
Rnd 14 *Sc in next 12 sts, 2 sc in next st; rep from * around—84 sc.
Rnd 15 *Sc in next 13 sts, 2 sc in next st; rep from * around—90 sc.
Rnd 16 *Sc in next 14 sts, 2 sc in next st; rep from * around—96 sc.
Rnd 17 *Sc in next 15 sts, 2 sc in next st; rep from * around—102 sc.
Rnd 18 *Sc in next 16 sts, 2 sc in next st; rep from * around—108 sc.

Encantada Crochet Bag

Rnd 19 *Sc in next 17 sts, 2 sc in next st; rep from * around—114 sc.
Rnd 20 *Sc in next 18 sts, 2 sc in next st; rep from * around—120 sc.
Rnd 21 *Sc in next 19 sts, 2 sc in next st; rep from * around—126 sc.
Rnd 22 *Sc in next 20 sts, 2 sc in next st; rep from * around—132 sc.
Rnd 23 *Sc in next 21 sts, 2 sc in next st; rep from * around—138 sc.
Rnd 24 *Sc in next 22 sts, 2 sc in next st; rep from * around—144 sc.
Rnds 25–27 Sc in each st around.

Body

Rnd 1 Working sc in each sc, following Row 1 of Color Chart, rep the 18 sts of the Chart 8 times around.
Rnds 2–54 Continuing to follow chart, sc in each st around.
Eyelet Rnd 55 Following chart, sc in first 11 sts, (ch 3, sk next 3 sts [eyelet made], sc in next 15 sts) 7 times, ch 3, sk next 3 sts, sc in last 4 sts—8 ch-3 sps (eyelets) and 120 sc.
Rnd 56 Following chart, sc in first 11 sts, (3 sc in next ch-3 sp, sc in next 11 sts) 9 times, 3 sc in next ch-3 sp, sc in last 4 sts—144 sc.
Rnds 57–63 Sc in each st around, following chart.
Fasten off.

Drawstring

Note For a wider drawstring, work additional rows of sc.
With A, make a chain approx 60"/152.5cm long.
Row 1 Sc in 2nd ch from hook and each ch across. Fasten off.

FINISHING

Weave drawstring in and out of eyelets, having ends of drawstring to RS of Bag. Following diagram, sew ends of drawstring to Bag.

Weave in ends. •

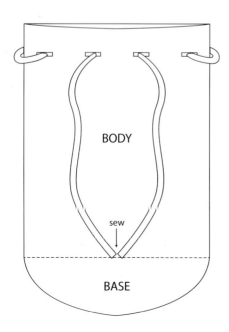

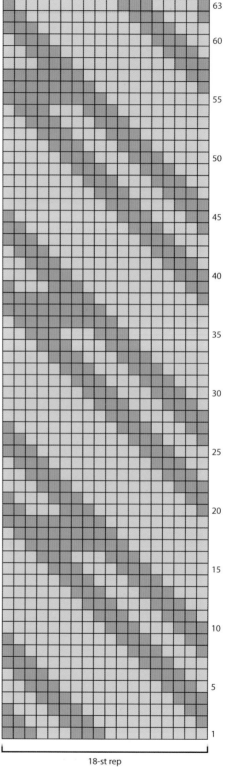

COLOR KEY

A

B

18-st rep
(rep 8 times around)

Dallas Tote

Easy

MEASUREMENTS
Circumference (at top edge after pleating) Approx 32"/81.5cm
Height (excluding strap) Approx 12"/30.5cm

MATERIALS
LION BRAND® Jeans®, 3½oz/100g balls, each approx 246yd/225m
(acrylic) (4)
• 2 balls in #153 Stovepipe (A)
• 1 ball each in #108 Brand New (B) and #121 Top Stitch (C)

Hook
• One size H-8 (5mm) crochet hook, *or size to obtain gauge*

Notions
• Stitch markers
• Tapestry needle

GAUGE
16 sc = approx 4"/10cm using size H-8 (5mm) crochet hook.
BE SURE TO CHECK YOUR GAUGE.

NOTES
1) Body of the Tote is made in one piece.
2) The yarn color is changed to make stripes. To change yarn color,
work last st of old color to last yarn over. Yarn over with new color
and draw through all loops on hook to complete st. Proceed with new
color. Fasten off old color.
3) Strap is worked separately then sewn to Tote.
4) Diagrams are provided to clarify the construction of the Tote.

TOTE
First Side
With C, ch 81.
Row 1 (RS) Sc in 2nd ch from hook and in each ch across and
change to A in last st—80 sc.
Row 2 With A, ch 1, turn, sc in each st across.
Row 3 With A, ch 3 (counts as dc), turn, dc in next sc and in each
sc across.
Rows 4–19 With A, rep Rows 2 and 3 eight times; change to C in
last st of Row 19.
Row 20 With C, rep Row 2.

Row 21 With C, ch 1, turn, sl st in each st across and change to B in
last st.
Rows 22–31 With B, rep Rows 2 and 3 five times; change to C in
last st of Row 31.
Rows 32 and 33 With C, rep Rows 20 and 21; change to A in
last st of Row 33.
Rows 34–43 With A, rep Rows 2 and 3 five times; change to C in
last st of Row 43.
Rows 44 and 45 With C, rep Rows 20 and 21.
Fasten off.

Second Side
Row 1 (RS) From RS and working along opposite side of foundation
ch, join C with sc in ch at base of first sc, sc in each ch across and
change to A in last st—80 sc.
Rows 2–45 Rep Rows 2–45 of first side.
Fasten off.

Dallas Tote

Strap

With C, ch 101.

Row 1 With C, working in back bumps of ch only, sc in 2nd ch from hook and in each ch across—100 sc.

Row 2 With C, ch 1, turn, sl st in each st across and change to B in last st.

Row 3 With B, ch 1, turn, sc in each st across.

Row 4 With B, ch 1, turn, sl st in each st across and change to A in last st.

Rows 5 and 6 With A, rep Rows 3 and 4; change to C in last st of Row 6.

Rows 7 and 8 With C, rep Rows 3 and 4.

Row 9 With C, rep Row 3.

Fasten off.

FINISHING

Assemble tote as follows:

Step 1 Fold Tote in half along foundation chain.

Step 2 Sew side seams, matching stripes.

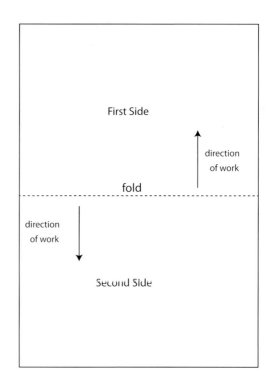

STEPS 1 & 2

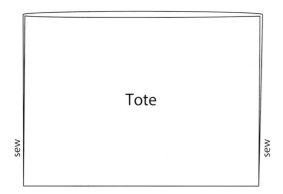

STEP 3

STEP 4

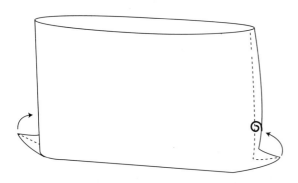

STEP 5

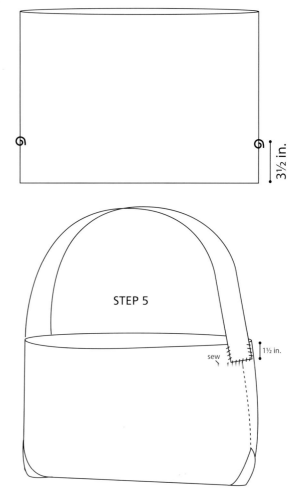

Step 3 Place a marker on each side seam, about 3½"/9cm above lower corners.

Step 4 On the RS, fold each lower corner up to the marker, forming a triangle. Sew the tip of each corner triangle to the Tote at markers.

Step 5 Sew ends of Strap to RS of top of Tote, about 1½"/4cm below top edge.

Step 6 Fold a pleat in Tote fabric on each side of Strap end, bringing folded edge of pleats to meet at center of Strap. Sew pleats in place.

Weave in ends.●

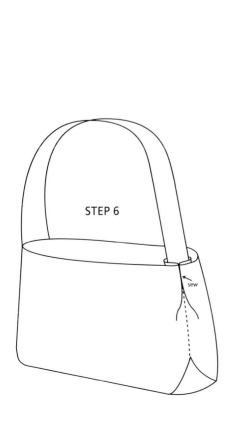

STEP 6

sew

Kaye Market Bag

Easy

MEASUREMENTS
Approx 11 x 12.5"/28 x 31.5cm, excluding handles

MATERIALS

Yarn
LION BRAND® Re-Up®, 2½oz/70g balls, each approx 114yd/105m
(cotton/polyester) (4)
• 1 ball each in #133 Orange (A), #143 Lilac (C), #158 Sunflower (D),
and #170 Lime (E)
• 2 balls in #112 Raspberry (B)

Hook
• One size H-8 (5mm) crochet hook, *or size to obtain gauge*

Notions
• Tapestry needle

GAUGE
One Hexagon = approx 5½"/14cm across using size H-8 (5mm)
crochet hook.
BE SURE TO CHECK YOUR GAUGE.

STITCH GLOSSARY
3-dc Cl (3 double crochet cluster) Yarn over, insert hook in
indicated st, yarn over and draw up a loop, yarn over and draw
through 2 loops on hook (2 loops rem on hook), [yarn over, insert
hook in same st, yarn over and draw up a loop, yarn over and draw
through 2 loops on hook] 2 times (4 loops rem on hook) yarn over
and draw through all loops on hook.

4-dc Cl (4 double crochet cluster) Yarn over, insert hook in
indicated st, yarn over and draw up a loop, yarn over and draw
through 2 loops on hook (2 loops rem on hook), [yarn over, insert
hook in same st, yarn over and draw up a loop, yarn over and draw
through 2 loops on hook] 3 times (5 loops rem on hook) yarn over,
draw through all loops on hook.

NOTES
1) Bag is made from 10 Hexagons, 2 each of 5 different color
combinations.

2) Hexagons are worked in the rnd with RS facing at all times. Do *not*
turn at the ends of rnds.

3) Handles are worked in rnds of sc, after the Hexagons have been
sewn tog.

BAG

Hexagon I (make 2)
With A, ch 6; join with sl st in first ch to form a ring.
Rnd 1 (RS) Ch 2, 3-dc Cl in ring, [ch 3, 4-dc Cl in ring] 5 times, ch 3;
join with sl st in top of first cluster—6 clusters at the end of this rnd.
Fasten off A.
Rnd 2 With RS facing, join B with sl st in any ch-3 sp, ch 2, [3-dc Cl,
ch 3, 4-dc Cl] in same ch-3 sp (corner made), *ch 3, [4-dc Cl, ch 3,
4-dc Cl] in next ch-3 sp (corner made); rep from * 4 more times, ch 3;
join with sl st in top of first cluster—12 clusters at the end of this rnd.
Fasten off B.
Rnd 3 With RS facing, join C with sl st in any corner ch-3 sp, ch 2,
[3-dc Cl, ch 3, 4-dc Cl] in same ch-3 sp (corner made), ch 3, 4-dc Cl
in next ch-3 sp, *ch 3, [4-dc Cl, ch 3, 4-dc Cl] in next ch-3 sp (corner
made), ch 3, 4-dc Cl in next ch-3 sp; rep from * 4 more times, ch 3;
join with sl st in top of first cluster—18 clusters at the end of this rnd.
Fasten off C.
Note In next rnd, take care to work dc as instructed, not clusters.
Rnd 4 With RS facing, join D with sl st in any corner ch-3 sp, ch 3
(counts as first dc), [2 dc, ch 2, 3 dc] in same ch-3 sp, 3 dc in each
of next 2 ch-3 sps, *[3 dc, ch 2, 3 dc] in next corner ch-3 sp, 3 dc in
each of next 2 ch-3 sps; rep from * 4 more times; join with sl st in top
of beg ch—72 dc at the end of this rnd.
Fasten off.

Hexagon II (make 2)
Make same as Hexagon I, using B for Rnd 1, C for Rnd 2, D for Rnd 3,
and E for Rnd 4.

Hexagon III (make 2)
Make same as Hexagon I, using C for Rnd 1, D for Rnd 2, E for Rnd 3,
and A for Rnd 4.

Hexagon IV (make 2)
Make same as Hexagon I, using D for Rnd 1, E for Rnd 2, A for Rnd 3,
and B for Rnd 4.

Hexagon V (make 2)
Make same as Hexagon I, using E for Rnd 1, A for Rnd 2, B for Rnd 3,
and C for Rnd 4.

FINISHING
Following Assembly Diagram, whipstitch the Hexagons tog. Fold piece
along dashed lines, matching A with B, and C with D. Whipstitch side
seams.

Handles

From RS, join B with a sl st in side seam between Hexagons I and III.
Rnd 1 Ch 1, *work 14 sc evenly spaced across side of Hexagon III to ch-2 sp at top point, ch 72, beg at ch-2 sp at point of Hexagon I, work 14 sc evenly spaced across side of Hexagon I to side seam (first handle made); rep from * for 2nd handle; join with sl st in first sc—144 ch and 56 sc.
Rnd 2 Ch 1, sc in each sc and ch around; join with sl st in first sc.
Rnds 3 and 4 Ch 1, sc in each sc around; join with sl st in first sc. Fasten off.

Edging

From RS, join B with sl st in any st on inside edge of first handle. Work sc evenly spaced around inside edge of handle and top edge of Bag; join with sl st in first sc. Fasten off.
Rep edging on 2nd handle.

Weave in ends. •

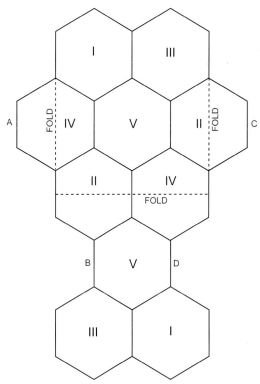

Striped Backpack

Easy

MEASUREMENTS
Approx 17 x 18"/43 x 46cm

MATERIALS
Yarn
LION BRAND® Wool-Ease® Thick & Quick®, 6oz/170g balls, each approx 106yd/97m (acrylic/wool) **6**
• 3 balls in #112 Raspberry (A)
• 1 ball in #178 Cilantro (B)

Hook
• One size N-13 (9mm) crochet hook, *or size to obtain gauge*

Notions
• Stitch marker
• Tapestry needle

GAUGE
9 sc + 8 rnds = 4"/10cm using size N-13 (9mm) crochet hook.
BE SURE TO CHECK YOUR GAUGE.

BACKPACK
Body
With A, ch 4, join with sl st in first ch to form a ring.
Rnd 1 Work 8 sc in ring, join with sl st in beg sc. Place marker for beg of rnd, move marker up as each rnd is completed.
Rnd 2 Ch 1, work 2 sc in each sc around, join with sl st in beg ch—16 sc.
Rnd 3 Ch 1, *sc in next sc, 2 sc in next sc; rep from * around—24 sc, join with sl st in beg ch.
Rnd 4 Ch 1, *sc in each of next 2 sc, 2 sc in next sc; rep from * around; join with sl st in beg ch—32 sc.
Rnd 5 Ch 1, *sc in each of next 3 sc, 2 sc in next sc; rep from * around; join with sl st in beg ch—40 sc.
Rnd 6 Ch 1, *sc in each of next 4 sc, 2 sc in next sc; rep from * around; join with sl st in beg ch—48 sc.
Rnd 7 Ch 1, *sc in each of next 5 sc, 2 sc in next sc; rep from * around; join with sl st in beg ch—56 sc.
Rnd 8 Ch 1, *sc in each of next 6 sc, 2 sc in next sc; rep from * around; join with sl st in beg ch—64 sc.
Rnd 9 Ch 1, *sc in each of next 7 sc, 2 sc in next sc; rep from * around; join with sl st in beg ch—72 sc.

Rnd 10 Ch 1, *sc in each of next 8 sc, 2 sc in next sc; rep from * around; join with sl st in beg ch—80 sc.
Rnds 11–17 Ch 1, sc in each sc around; join with sl st in beg ch—80 sc.
At end of Rnd 17, fasten off A.
Rnd 18 Join B with sl st, ch 1, sc in each sc around, join with sl st in beg ch.
Rnds 19–25 With B, ch 1, sc in each sc around, join with sl st in beg ch.
At end of Rnd 25, fasten off B.
Rnd 26 Join A with sl st, ch 1, sc in each sc around, join with sl st in beg ch.
Rnds 27–29 With A, ch 1, sc in each sc around, join with sl st in beg ch.
Eyelet Rnd 30 Ch 3, skip first 2 sc, *sc in each of next 3 sc, ch 2, skip next 2 sc; rep from * 14 times more, end sc in each of last 3 sc, join with sl st in first ch of beg ch.
Rnd 31 Ch 1, sc in each sc, working 2 sc in each ch-2 space around—80 sc.
Rnds 32–33 Ch 1, sc in each sc around, join with sl st in beg ch. Fasten off.

Cord
With A, ch 2, join with sl st in beg ch.
Work in a continuous spiral as follows: *work 1 sl st in next st; rep from * until Cord measures 60"/152.5cm. Fasten off.
Weave cord through eyelets of Rnd 30, with both cord ends emerging on right side. Mark center point between cords. Pull cord ends through from right to wrong side of Backpack at center point just below B stripe. Knot cord ends securely on inside of Backpack.

FINISHING
Weave in ends.•

Golightly Tote

Easy

MEASUREMENTS
Circumference (at widest point) Approx 35"/89cm

MATERIALS
Yarn
LION BRAND® Vanna's Glamour®, 1¾oz/50g balls, each approx 202yd/185m (acrylic/other) 🟦
• 3 balls each in #100 Diamond (A) and #150 Platinum (B)

Hook
• One size I-9 (5.5mm) crochet hook, *or size to obtain gauge*

Notions
• Tapestry needle

GAUGE
12 dc = 4"/10cm over pattern with 1 strand each of A and B held tog using size I-9 (5.5mm) hook.
BE SURE TO CHECK YOUR GAUGE.

STITCH GLOSSARY
dc2tog (dc dec) Yo, insert hook in sp between next 2 sts and draw up a loop, yo and draw through 2 loops; yo, insert hook in next sp and draw up a loop, yo and draw through 2 loops; yo and draw through all loops on hook.

NOTES
1) Work dc into sps between st, rather than into sts.
2) Tote is worked with 1 strand each of A and B held tog throughout.

TOTE
With 1 strand each of A and B held tog, ch 3; join with sl st in first ch to form a ring.
Rnd 1 Ch 3 (counts as first dc here and throughout), work 11 more dc in ring; join with sl st in sp between beg ch and next dc—12 dc.
Rnd 2 Ch 3, turn, dc in same sp as join, *2 dc in next sp between sts; rep from * around; join with sl st in sp between beg ch and next dc—24 dc.
Rnd 3 Ch 3, turn, dc in same sp as join, dc in next sp between sts, *2 dc in next sp between sts, dc in next sp between sts; rep from * around; join with sl st in sp between beg ch and next dc—36 dc.
Rnd 4 Ch 3, turn, dc in same sp as join, dc in next 2 sps between sts, *2 dc in next sp between sts, dc in next 2 sps between sts; rep from *

around; join with sl st in sp between beg ch and next dc—48 dc.
Rnd 5 Ch 3, turn, dc in same sp as join, dc in next 3 sps between sts, *2 dc in next sp between sts, dc in next 3 sps between sts; rep from * around; join with sl st in sp between beg ch and next dc—60 dc.
Rnd 6 Ch 3, turn, dc in each sp around; join with sl st in sp between beg ch and next dc.
Rnd 7 Ch 3, turn, dc in same sp as join, dc in next 4 sps between sts, *2 dc in next sp between sts, dc in next 4 sps between sts; rep from * around; join with sl st in sp between beg ch and next dc—72 dc.
Rnd 8 Ch 3, turn, dc in same sp as join, dc in next 7 sps between sts, *2 dc in next sp between sts, dc in next 7 sps between sts; rep from * around; join with sl st in sp between beg ch and next dc—81 dc.
Rnd 9 Ch 3, turn, dc in same sp as join, dc in next 8 sps between sts, *2 dc in next sp between sts, dc in next 8 sps between sts; rep from * around; join with sl st in sp between beg ch and next dc—90 dc.
Rnd 10 Ch 3, turn, dc in same sp as join, dc in next 9 sps between sts, *2 dc in next sp between sts, dc in next 9 sps between sts; rep from * around; join with sl st in sp between beg ch and next dc—99 dc.
Rnds 11–22 Rep Rnd 6.
Rnd 23 Ch 3, turn, dc in next 30 sps between sts, dc2tog, *dc in next 31 sps between sts, dc2tog; rep from * once more; join with sl st in sp between beg ch and next dc—96 dc.
Rnd 24 Rep Rnd 6.
Rnd 25 Ch 3, turn, dc in next 29 sps between sts, dc2tog, *dc in next 30 sps between sts, dc2tog; rep from * once more; join with sl st in sp between beg ch and next dc—93 dc.
Rnd 26 Rep Rnd 6.
Rnd 27 Ch 3, turn, dc in next 28 sps between sts, dc2tog, *dc in next 29 sps between sts, dc2tog; rep from * once more; join with sl st in sp between beg ch and next dc—90 dc.
Rnd 28 Rep Rnd 6. Do *not* fasten off.

Handles
Row 29 Ch 3, dc2tog, dc in next 29 sps, dc2tog, dc in next sp; leave remaining sts unworked—33 sts.
Rows 30–41 Ch 3, turn, dc2tog, dc in each sp across to last 3 sps, dc2tog, dc in next sp—9 sts.
Rows 42–48 Ch 3, turn, dc in each sp across—9 sts. Fasten off at end of Row 48.
Skip 10 sps from last st worked on Rnd 29. Join 1 strand each of A and B with sl st in next sp, ch 3 and work same as for first handle. Do *not* fasten off. From wrong side, sc ends of handles tog. Do *not* fasten off

FINISHING
With 1 strand each of A and B held tog, sc evenly around edge of handle. Fasten off.
From right side, join 1 strand each of A and B held tog with sl st at opposite end of handle seam. Sc evenly around edge of handle. Fasten off. Weave in ends.•

Granny Square Market Bag

Easy

MEASUREMENTS
Approx 12"/30.5cm square

MATERIALS
Yarn
LION BRAND® Vanna's Choice®, 3½oz/100g balls, each approx 170yd/156m (acrylic/rayon) (4)
• 1 ball each in #107 Sapphire (A) and #130 Honey (B)

Hook
• One size J-10 (6mm) crochet hook, *or size to obtain gauge*

Notions
• Tapestry needle

GAUGE
Rnds 1–4 = approx 5"/12.5cm using size J-10 (6mm) crochet hook.
BE SURE TO CHECK YOUR GAUGE.

NOTES
1) Bag is made from two large Granny Squares crocheted tog on three sides.
2) To keep Granny Squares even, join new color in a different corner each time the color is changed.
3) After the squares are joined, the Handle is sewn to the top open edge of the Bag and a crocheted edging is worked around top edge of Bag and sides of Handle.

BAG
Square (make 2)
With A, ch 4; join with sl st in first ch to form a ring.
Rnd 1 Ch 3 (counts as dc here and throughout this pattern), 2 dc in ring, ch 2, [3 dc in ring, ch 2] 3 times; join with sl st in top of beg ch.
Rnd 2 With A, ch 4 (counts as dc, ch-1 here and throughout this pattern), *[3 dc, ch 2, 3 dc] in next ch-2 sp (corner made), ch 1; rep from * 2 more times, [3 dc, ch 2, 2 dc] in next corner ch-2 sp; join with sl st in 3rd ch of beg ch-4. Fasten off.
Rnd 3 Join B with sl st in any corner ch-2 sp, ch 3, [2 dc, ch 2, 3 dc] in same ch-2 sp, ch 1, 3 dc in next ch-1 sp, ch 1, *[3 dc, ch 2, 3 dc] in next corner ch-2 sp, ch 1, 3 dc in next ch-1 sp, ch 1; rep from * 2 more times; join with sl st in top of beg ch.
Rnd 4 With B, ch 4, [3 dc, ch 2, 3 dc] in next corner ch-2 sp, ch 1, *[3 dc in next ch-1 sp, ch 1] to next corner ch-2 sp, [3 dc, ch 2, 3 dc] in next corner ch-2 sp, ch 1; rep from * 2 more times, 3 dc in next ch-1 sp, ch 1, 2 dc in last ch-1 sp; join with sl st in 3rd ch of beg ch-4. Fasten off.
Rnd 5 Join A with sl st in any corner ch-2 sp, ch 3, [2 dc, ch 2, 3 dc] in same ch-2 sp, ch 1, [3 dc in next ch-1 sp, ch 1] to next corner ch-2 sp, *[3 dc, ch 2, 3 dc] in next ch-2 sp, ch 1, [3 dc in next ch-1 sp, ch 1] to next corner ch-2 sp; rep from * 2 more times; join with sl st in top of beg ch.
Rnd 6 With A, ch 4, [3 dc, ch 2, 3 dc] in next corner ch-2 sp, ch 1, *[3 dc in next ch-1 sp, ch 1] to next corner ch-2 sp, [3 dc, ch 2, 3 dc] in next corner ch-2 sp, ch 1; rep from * 2 more times, [3 dc in next ch-1 sp, ch 1] to last ch-1 sp, 2 dc in last ch-1 sp; join with sl st in 3rd ch of beg ch-4. Fasten off.
Rnds 7 and 8 With B, rep Rnds 5 and 6.
Rnds 9 and 10 With A, rep Rnds 5 and 6.
Fasten off.

Handle
With A, ch 73.
Row 1 Sc in 2nd ch from hook, and in each ch across—72 sts.
Rows 2 and 3 Ch 1, turn, sc in each sts across.
Fasten off.

FINISHING
Hold Squares with WS tog.
Row 1 Working through both Squares, join B with a sl st in any corner ch-2 sp, sc in each sc and ch around 3 sides of Squares, leaving remaining side open for top. Fasten off.
Sew ends of Handle to top of Bag.

Top Edging
With RS facing, join B with a sl st anywhere along top edge of Bag.
Rnd 1 Sc evenly spaced across top edge of Bag and along side edge of Handle. Fasten off.
Rep edging on opposite side of Handle and top of Bag.

Weave in ends. •

Pensacola Bag

Easy

MEASUREMENTS
Circumference Approx 38"/96.5cm
Height (including straps) Approx 21"/53.5cm

MATERIALS
Yarn
LION BRAND® Rewind, 3½oz/100g balls, each approx 219yd/200m (polyester/viscose) (5)
• 2 balls in #123 Greige

Hook
• One size K-10½ (6.5mm) crochet hook, *or size to obtain gauge*

Notion
• Tapestry needle

GAUGE
13 sc = approx 4"/10cm using size K-10½ (6.5mm) crochet hook.
BE SURE TO CHECK YOUR GAUGE.

STITCH GLOSSARY
beg-Cl (beginning cluster) Ch 3, yarn over, insert hook in indicated st and draw up a loop, yarn over and draw through 2 loops on hook (2 loops rem on hook); yarn over, insert hook in same st and draw up a loop, yarn over and draw through 2 loops on hook, yarn over and draw through all 3 loops on hook.

Cl (cluster) Yarn over, insert hook in indicated st, yarn over and draw up a loop, yarn over and draw through 2 loops on hook (2 loops rem on hook), [yarn over, insert hook in same st, yarn over and draw up a loop, yarn over and draw through 2 loops on hook] twice; yarn over and draw through all 4 loops on hook.

NOTES
1) Bag is worked in one piece, in 3 sections: Base, body, and straps.
2) All sections are worked in joined rnds with right side always facing.

BAG
Base
Ch 4; join with a sl st in first ch to make a ring.
Rnd 1 Ch 1, make 6 sc in ring; sl st in first sc to join.
Rnd 2 Ch 1, work 2 sc in each of the 6 sc around; join with sl st in first sc—you will have 12 sc in this rnd.

Note Always work the first st of each rnd in the same st as the join.
Rnd 3 Ch 1, *sc in next st, 2 sc in next st; rep from * around; join with sl st in first sc—18 sc.
Rnd 4 Ch 1, *sc in next 2 sts, 2 sc in next st; rep from * around; join with sl st in first sc—24 sc.
Rnd 5 Ch 1, *sc in next 3 sts, 2 sc in next st; rep from * around; join with sl st in first sc—30 sc.
Rnd 6 Ch 1, *sc in next 4 sts, 2 sc in next st; rep from * around; join with sl st in first sc—36 sc.
Rnd 7 Ch 1, *sc in next 5 sts, 2 sc in next st; rep from * around; join with sl st in first sc—42 sc.
Rnd 8 Ch 1, *sc in next 6 sts, 2 sc in next st; rep from * around; join with sl st in first sc—48 sc.
Rnd 9 Ch 1, *sc in next 7 sts, 2 sc in next st; rep from * around; join with sl st in first sc—54 sc.
Rnd 10 Ch 1, *sc in next 8 sts, 2 sc in next st; rep from * around; join with sl st in first sc—60 sc.
Rnd 11 Ch 1, *sc in next 9 sts, 2 sc in next st; rep from * around; join with sl st in first sc—66 sc.
Rnd 12 Ch 1, *sc in next 10 sts, 2 sc in next st; rep from * around; join with sl st in first sc—72 sc.

Rnd 13 Ch 1, *sc in next 11 sts, 2 sc in next st; rep from * around; join with sl st in first sc—78 sc.

Rnd 14 Ch 1, *sc in next 12 sts, 2 sc in next st; rep from * around; join with sl st in first sc—84 sc.

Rnd 15 Ch 1, *sc in next 13 sts, 2 sc in next st; rep from * around; join with sl st in first sc—90 sc.

Rnd 16 Ch 1, *sc in next 14 sts, 2 sc in next st; rep from * around; join with sl st in first sc—96 sc.

Rnd 17 Ch 1, *sc in next 15 sts, 2 sc in next st; rep from * around; join with sl st in first sc—102 sc.

Rnd 18 Ch 1, *sc in next 16 sts, 2 sc in next st; rep from * around; join with sl st in first sc—108 sc.

Rnd 19 Ch 1, *sc in next 17 sts, 2 sc in next st; rep from * around; join with sl st in first sc—114 sc.

Rnd 20 Ch 1, *sc in next 18 sts, 2 sc in next st; rep from * around; join with sl st in first sc—120 sc.

Body

Rnd 1 Beg-Cl in same st as join, *ch 1, skip next st, Cl in next st; rep from * to last st, ch 1, skip last st; join with sl st in top of beg ch-3— you'll have 60 clusters and 60 ch-1 sps.

Rnd 2 Ch 1, 2 sc in each ch-1 sp around; join with sl st in first sc—120 sc.

Rnds 3–8 Ch 1, sc in each sc around; join with sl st in first sc. Rep Rnds 1–8 twice more, then rep Rnds 1–5.

Straps

Set-Up Rnd Ch 1, sc in next 15 sts, ch 55, skip next 30 sts for first strap, sc in next 30 sts, ch 55, skip next 30 sts for second strap, sc in last 15 sts; join with sl st in first sc—you'll have 60 sc and 2 ch-55 sps.

Next Rnd Ch 1, sc in each sc and ch around; join with sl st in first sc—170 sc.

Last 3 Rnds Ch 1, sc in each st around; join with sl st in first sc. Fasten off.

FINISHING

Weave in ends.•

Bucket Tote

Easy

MEASUREMENTS
Circumference Approx 18"/45.5cm
Length (excluding strap) Approx 13"/33cm

MATERIALS
Yarn
LION BRAND® Wool-Ease® Thick & Quick®, 6oz/170g balls, each approx 106yd/97m (acrylic/wool) **(6)**
• 3 balls in #099 Fisherman

Hook
• One size N-13 (9mm) crochet hook, *or size to obtain gauge*

Notions
• Stitch markers
• Tapestry needle

GAUGE
10½ sts = approx 4"/10cm using size N-13 (9mm) crochet hook.
BE SURE TO CHECK YOUR GAUGE.

STITCH GLOSSARY
Flower-spike st
NOTES
1) Each Flower-spike st is made by drawing up 5 loops in sts of previous rnds.
2) When drawing up a loop in a st of a previous rnd, elongate the loop enough so that it lies flat against your work.
3) Instructions for working the Flower-spike assume that you are working from right to left. If you are working from left to right, simply change all references to "right" to "left" and vice versa.

STEPS
1) Count down 2 rnds and then 2 sts to the right of the next st, insert your hook into this st and draw up a loop—2 loops on hook.
2) Move one st to the left and one rnd down (3 rnds below the current rnd), insert your hook into this st and draw up a loop—3 loops on hook.
3) Move one st to the left (you are now directly under the next st) and one more rnd down (4 rnds below the current rnd), insert your hook into this st and draw up a loop—4 loops on hook.

4) Move one st to the left and one rnd up (3 rnds below the current rnd), insert your hook into this st and draw up a loop—5 loops on hook.
5) Move one st to the left and one rnd up (2 rnds below the current rnd), insert your hook into this st and draw up a loop—6 loops on hook.
6) Yarn over and draw through all loops on hook to make Flower-spike st.
7) When you continue on with the rnd, skip the next st, the st under which you worked the Flower-spike st.

NOTES
1) Tote is worked in continuous rnds with RS facing at all times. Do *not* join or turn unless otherwise noted.
2) Tote is worked from the base up to the top. The strap is worked directly onto the Tote.
3) We suggest you read carefully through the instructions before beginning the strap. The strap is easy, but the construction is slightly unusual.
4) Once both halves of the strap have been completed, strap is folded and seamed. This makes an extra sturdy strap!

TOTE
Body
Ch 4; join with a sl st in first ch to form a ring.
Rnd 1 (RS) Work 6 sc in ring. Place marker in first st for beg of rnd and move marker up as each rnd is completed.
Rnd 2 Work 2 sc in each sc around—12 sc at the end of this rnd.
Rnd 3 *Sc in next sc, 2 sc in next sc; rep from * around—18 sc
Rnd 4 *Sc in each of next 2 sc, 2 sc in next sc; rep from * around—24 sc.
Rnd 5 *Sc in each of next 3 sc, 2 sc in next sc; rep from * around—30 sc.
Rnd 6 *Sc in each of next 4 sc, 2 sc in next sc; rep from * around—36 sc.
Rnd 7 *Sc in each of next 5 sc, 2 sc in next sc; rep from * around—42 sc.
Rnd 8 *Sc in each of next 6 sc, 2 sc in next sc; rep from * around—48 sc.
Rnds 9–13 Sc in each sc around.
Rnd 14 *Sc in each of next 7 sc, Flower-spike st in next sc; rep from * around—42 sc and 6 Flower-spikes.
Rnds 15–17 Sc in each sc around.
Rnd 18 Sc in next 4 sc, Flower-spike st in next sc, *sc in next 7 sc, Flower-spike st in next sc; rep from * to last 3 sc, sc in last 3 sc—42 sc and 6 Flower-spikes.
Rnd 19 Sc in each sc around.
Rep Rnd 19 until Tote measures 13"/33cm from beginning.

Strap

FIRST HALF

Rnd 1 (RS) Sc in next 24 sc, then work a ch approx 29"/73.5cm long; leave the last 24 sc unworked for now, you'll return to these sts to make the other side of the strap. Join the end of the ch with a sl st to the first of the 24 sc you worked at the beg of this rnd.

Rnd 2 Sc in 24 sc of Rnd 1, placing a marker between the 3rd and 4th sc and a second marker between the 21st and 22nd sc, sc in each ch of strap.

Note When working sl sts in next 3 rnds, take care to carefully insert your hook under the top 2 loops of sts of previous rnd.

Note On Rnd 3, move each marker outwards 1 st to add 2 more sts between markers.

Rnd 3 Sc in each sc around to one st before marker, reposition marker, moving it 1 st outwards to have 1 more st between markers, sl st in each st to next marker, remove marker, sl st in next st and replace marker, sc in each sc to end of rnd.

Rnds 4 and 5 Rep Rnd 3, moving markers outwards by 1 st rnd.
Fasten off.

SECOND HALF

Rnd 1 (RS) With RS facing, join yarn with sc in first unworked st at top of Tote, sc in next 23 sc, place a marker between the 3rd and 4th sc and another marker between the 21st and 22nd sc; working across opposite side of strap foundation ch, sc in each ch across strap.
Rep Rnds 3–5 of first half of strap.
Fasten off, leaving a long yarn tail for sewing.
Remove markers. Fold strap in half and with yarn tail, sew long sides of strap together.

FINISHING

Weave in ends. •

Trenton Tote

●●●
Easy

MEASUREMENTS
Circumference Approx 26"/66cm
Height (excluding handles) Approx 13½"/34.5cm

MATERIALS
Yarn
LION BRAND® 24/7 Cotton®, 3½oz/100g balls, each approx
186yd/170m (mercerized cotton)
• 2 balls in #172 Grass

Hook
• One size I-9 (5.5mm) crochet hook, *or size to obtain gauge*

Notions
• Stitch marker
• Tapestry needle

GAUGE
Exact gauge is not essential to this project.

NOTES
1) Base of Bag is worked in joined rnds with RS always facing. Do *not* turn at the beg of rnds of base.
2) Sides of Bag are worked in joined and turned rnds in a Diamond Lattice pattern. When working sides, turn at the beg of every rnd.
3) Top edge and straps are worked in a continuous spiral. Do join and do *not* turn at the beg of rnds.

TOTE
Base
Ch 3, join with sl st in first ch to form a ring.
Rnd 1 Ch 1, work 8 sc in ring; join with sl st in first sc—8 sc.
Rnd 2 Ch 1, work 2 sc in each st around; join with sl st in first sc—16 sc.
Rnd 3 Ch 1, [sc in next st, 2 sc in next st] 8 times; join with sl st in first sc—24 sc.
Rnd 4 Ch 1, [sc in next 2 sts, 2 sc in next st] 8 times; join with sl st in first sc—32 sc.
Rnd 5 Ch 1, [sc in next 3 sts, 2 sc in next st] 8 times; join with sl st in first sc—40 sc.
Rnd 6 Ch 1, [sc in next 4 sts, 2 sc in next st] 8 times; join with sl st in first sc—48 sc.

Rnd 7 Ch 1, [sc in next 5 sts, 2 sc in next st] 8 times; join with sl st in first sc—56 sc.
Rnd 8 Ch 1, [sc in next 6 sts, 2 sc in next st] 8 times; join with sl st in first sc—64 sc.
Rnd 9 Ch 1, [sc in next 7 sts, 2 sc in next st] 8 times; join with sl st in first sc—72 sc.
Rnd 10 Ch 1, [sc in next 8 sts, 2 sc in next st] 8 times; join with sl st in first—80 sc.
Rnd 11 Ch 1, [sc in next 9 sts, 2 sc in next st] 8 times; join with sl st in first sc—88 sc.
Rnd 12 Ch 1, [sc next 10 sts, 2 sc in next st] 8 times; join with sl st in first sc—96 sc.
Rnd 13 Ch 1, [sc in next 11 sts, 2 sc in next st] 8 times; join with sl st in first sc—104 sc.

Diamond Lattice Pattern
Rnd 1 (RS) Ch 1, sc in next 2 sts, *ch 5, skip next 3 sts, sc in next 5 sts; rep from * to last 6 sts, ch 5, skip next 3 sts, sc in last 3 sts; join with sl st in first sc—you will have 65 sc and 13 ch-5 sps in this rnd.
Rnd 2 (WS) Ch 1, turn, sc in first 2 sc, ch 3, sc in next ch-5 sp, *ch 3, sk next sc, sc in next 3 sc, ch 3, sc in next ch-5 sp; rep from * to last 2 sc, ch 3, sc in last 2 sc; join with sl st in first sc—53 sc and 26 ch-3 sps.
Rnd 3 Ch 1, turn, sc in first sc, *ch 3, sc in next ch-3 sp, sc in next sc, sc in next ch-3 sp, ch 3, sk next sc, sc in next sc; rep from * around; join with sl st in first sc—53 sc and 26 ch-3 sps.
Rnd 4 Ch 7 (counts as tr, ch 3), turn, sc in next ch-3 sp, sc in next 3 sc, sc in next ch-3 sp, *ch 5, sc in next ch-3 sp, sc in next 3 sc, sc in next ch-3 sp; rep from * to last sc, ch 3, tr in last sc; join with sl st in 4th ch of beg ch-7—2 tr, 65 sc, 2 ch-3 sps and 12 ch-5 sps.
Rnd 5 Ch 1, turn, sc in first tr, ch 3, sk first ch-3 sp, sk next sc, sc in next 3 sc, *ch 3, sc in next ch-5 sp, ch 3, sk next sc, sc in next 3 sc; rep from * to last ch-sp, ch 3, sc in same ch as joining; join with sl st in first sc—53 sc and 26 ch-3 sps.
Rnd 6 Ch 1, turn, sc in first sc, sc next in ch-3 sp, ch 3, sk next sc, sc in next sc, *ch 3, sc in next ch-3 sp, sc in next sc, sc in next ch-3 sp, ch 3, sk next sc, sc in next sc; rep from * to last ch-3 sp, ch 3, sc in last ch-3 sp, sc in last sc; join with sl st in first sc—53 sc and 26 ch-3 sps.
Rnd 7 (RS) Ch 1, turn, sc in first 2 sc, sc in next ch-3 sp, ch 5, sc in next ch-3 sp, *sc in next 3 sc, sc in next ch-3 sp, ch 5, sc in next ch-3 sp; rep from * to last 2 sc, sc in last 2 sc; join with sl st in first sc—65 sc and 13 ch-5 sps.
Rep Rnds 2–7 until piece measures approx 10"/25.5cm from last rnd of base, end with a Rnd 7 as the last rnd you work.

Trenton Tote

Top Edge and Straps

Rnd 1 (RS) Ch 1, work 84 sc evenly spaced around top edge of Bag; do *not* join with a sl st, work in a continuous spiral—84 sts. Place marker for beg of rnd, move marker up as each rnd is completed.

Rnds 2–4 Sc in each sc around.

Rnd 5 Sc in next 15 sts, ch 50 for strap, sk next 12 sts, sc in next 30 sts, ch 50 for strap, sk next 12 sts, sc in last 15 sts.

Rnd 6 Sc in each sc and ch around—160 sc.

Rnds 7–9 Sc in each sc around.

Fasten off.

FINISHING

Weave in ends.•